Safer

Shekel HaKodesh

The philosopher

Rabbi

Yosef Kimchi

SimchatChaim.com

There is no known book without mistakes. Therefore, I ask in every language of application if anyone has any questions, comments, clarifications, corrections, please send to: <u>simchatchaim@yahoo.com</u>

All material used in this section may not be used for commercial purposes, but only for study and teaching.

To get this book or books and information Email me at:

<u>simchatchaim@yahoo.com</u>

Shekel HaKodesh

Rabbi

Yosef Kimchi

Contents of the Book

Shekel HaKodesh

Rabbi

Yosef Kimchi

The Book

The book **Shekel HaKodesh** is about the principles of the Jewish faith, the rabbi explains his words philosophically in a poetic and picturesque way. This book is a moral book and talks about Modesty Independence.

Yosef Kimhi [1105–1170] [Hebrew: יוסף קמחי] was a medieval Jewish rabbi and biblical commentator. He was the father of Moses and David Kimhi, and the teacher of Rabbi Menachem Ben Simeon and poet Joseph Zabara.

Grammarian, exegete, poet, and translator; born in southern Spain about 1105; died about 1170. Forced to leave his native country owing to the religious persecutions of the Almohades, who invaded the Iberian Peninsula in 1146, he settled in Narbonne, Provence, where he spent the rest of his life. The Hachmei Provence were under the considerable influence of the neighboring Spanish Jewish community to the south at the time.

His son David, though but a child at the time of his father's death, may also be considered one of his pupils, either directly through his works, or indirectly through the instruction David received from his elder brother Moses.

Shekel HaKodesh

Rabbi

Yosef Kimchi

Prelude

O wise one, lay it to heart at all times, yea, every day, whether weekday or feast-day, sabbath or new moon, and you will find in - **The Holy Shekel** every good quality, more precious than gold, yea, than fine gold. The object of this work is to make clear the proverb and parable, knowledge and counsel, the words of the wise and their dark sayings, the maxims of the sages and men of understanding, and their conceits.

I, Yosef the son of Itzhak, surnamed Kimchi, have weighed such in the balance of the Holy Tongue, measuring them in verses; I found them originally scattered here and there, some in Arabic, and some in Hebrew, and I have weighed them so that they may be easily understood, both as regards matter and language.

I have, therefore, called the book - **The Holy Shekel**, collecting the proverbs and maxims resembling one another, into their appropriate chapters; there are in all 22 chapters, according to the number of the letters of the Torah [Hebrew alphabet]. I have summed up the verses of each and every chapter at the end thereof, the number being contained in the similarly sounding final words of the concluding couplet - one line of which sets forth the subject matter, and the other the number of rhymes, for the benefit of those who would be wise and understand.

The wise will hear, and gather doctrine and speech, and the man of understanding will gain prudence.

Now, I say, the vital soul of Wisdom is beyond the heavens in duration. Take millstones from the mountains of Intelligence and grind therewith the flour of Thought and having made all due preparation for the sweet fare and rich repast, dress thy [spiritual] food and mix thy [ethereal] wine, so that their fragrance may be wafted as myrrh in every man's countenance.

Regard these rhymes well. There cannot be compared to them ornaments of the choicest gold, even of the gold of Parvaim; they are as rows of precious stones set in beauteous pattern of finest linen, a delight both to the eyes and the heart; I have arranged them in verse, weighing them not in the material balance, but balancing them in my mind, and this for the daughter of the son of Kimchi.

The sparks of burning instruction glow as a torch -
wherefore grasp them not with tongs but with the
heart. Such verses are written upon the tablet of the
heart of man; wherefore place thou them upon these
tablets.

bright, and thy soul shall be at ease with herself,
finding favour with all.

Finished with the help of God. Blessed be He who
giveth power to the weary, and to him who hath no
strength He increaseth strength.

Shekel HaKodesh

Rabbi

Yosef Kimchi

On Wisdom

Wisdom giveth life to its possessor, paying the reward of God for His service. By wisdom doth man acquire the days of this life, a goodly name, and honour after death.

The rain of Heaven reviveth the seed in the hour in which it falleth; but if it falls too heavily, it will surely kill the seed. Wisdom, too, the wise man's heart reviveth; but the more it groweth, the surer - T'will lead to eternal life.

Grieve not when thy wealth doth perish, if thy sense and honour remain; for why shouldst thou pine for the scabbard, when thy hand the sword doth retain?

Who is met to be king o'er the world, the ship as mariner or captain to guide? He who in all things is wise, is alert in deciding, enduring much in the search after wisdom.

Why should he who wisdom gathereth, he whose hand layeth hold of truth, fear the bear, the lion, or adder, the poison of dragon, or aught that doeth harm? Despond thou, if thy good sense doth fail, such loss will never be regained; wherefore keep thy sense for aye, once gone it will not come again.

The man whom God with much knowledge hath graced, need have no care for wealth or possessions; Tis peace that marketh the wise man's end; the end of wealth is bitter, and sad remorse.

Search thou for understanding, seek wisdom, and regard not the issue; investigate her hidden worth, her treasure-store, and beauty.

Verily, as a man without a wife is fear without wisdom; but wisdom without fear is as a woman without a spouse. Understanding without wisdom is as a bow without a string; but the man in whom these two are found will ever - **Rise from high to higher**.

No man is accounted great by reason of his body's strength, but according to the brilliance of his mind, his wisdom, and his prudence. Not he who wanteth bread doth want, who wisdom wanteth, wanteth much, he lacketh that which sustaineth life.

Lo, wisdom may indeed be found in the poor and

forlorn state, as well as in the abundance of this world's wealth and power; just as this field will produce all wheat, whilst the one adjoining will bring forth thorn and brier.

If - Tis wisdom which thou dost love, choose upright action, and hate rebellion. Know, wisdow is like a tree, action is its fruit. Wisdom [theory] to practice joined will lead a man to the day of his death; but knowledge, whence no actions flow [die with him], he leaveth no aftermath.

Choose the seat of the wise, and men will honour thee for thy good sense, and praise thee in full measure. When thou wouldst err, they will teach thee; and whensoever thou wouldst falter, they will make thee understand and direct thee in the right way.

Knowledge and action are twins by birth, one giving glory to the other. Action without understanding, how can it be pure? And where there is no action, what reward hath understanding?

I would rather leave wisdom through folly and lack of knowledge than, knowing what is right, forsake it in scorn.

A man, wise in his time, was once asked - How is it that thou excellest all others in wisdom? And he replied - I did not spend that which I had upon the juice of grape or wine, upon the midnight oil it was spent.

Truly man's body without wisdom is as a house without a base, as a field in which the thorn springeth forth in the furrow.

Canst, thou find a quality in man higher than that which recogniseth the measure of his position, so that when he speaketh, he will but speak to all men according to his rule and regulation?

A man of wisdom will continue in the search for wisdom, seeking knowledge wherever it may dwell or be kept. There is no fool equal to him who may think that he hath finished and completed his studies. Obtain wisdom, and say not that thou hast enough to sustain fully therewith the position thou dost hold; for know, that wealth without wisdom will be lost, so that it ceaseth to exist, and thou mayest remain bereft of all things; whilst he who laboureth in the search for wisdom, and stoopeth to search out and find one to enlighten him, may on the morrow be in the track of rising higher; and, having been the tail before, may rise to become the head.

Kings may rule the world, but the wise rule kings.

Men of understanding find delight in their wisdom, but fools delight in their folly.

Blindness of heart is blindness; indeed, therefore incline thou the ear to hearken; for what availeth the open eye, if the heart itself be closed?

How many men there are in the world who, as they make their appearance, strike terror; but when they once begin to speak, they are thought to be no better than dumb?

There are men of stature and height, men of muscle, able to brandish the spear and the lance; but of what avail are they without knowledge, being altogether lacking in understanding and wisdom?

If a thing be clearly good, let the man of wisdom take hold of it; if it clearly doth harm, let him move away from it; if it be doubtful whether it be good or ill, let him cast his burden upon the Lord.

A man who with wisdom humility doth join, will find that among all qualities it standeth pre-eminent. So also, will he be respected and honoured, who at all times joineth forgiveness with power.

The hard-working student whose constant aim it is to strengthen himself in his studies, even to tread in the path of wisdom, is not likely to be possessed of two things - a greasy face or portly body.

My son, if thou wouldst be wise, choose four things, and beware lest thou neglect the fifth - be learned; if this cannot be, be a learner, a listener, be law-loving, and be not too much given to bitterness.

In searching for wisdom at the hands of the wise, be not slow to ask questions. Be not ashamed to confess - **I know not**, if thou grasp not the depths of a matter. If thou dost overcome this sense of bashfulness, thou wilt in time be recognised and esteemed by those among whom thou dost move.

Exult not when men honour thee for thy wealth and power; for when thy honours flee from thee, then also will their flattery flee. Let it be most sweet to thee, if thou dost honour gain from that pre-eminence which moveth with thee, even when thou dost roam abroad. To him who enquireth. Who are the great ones of the world, the wise or the rich? Answer, He who carrieth about with him all that he hath, that which may sustain him, whether he cross the desert, or travel by sea.

Then say - Why dost thou find it is the way of the world for the wise to be knocking at the door of the rich? Because the wise of heart, knowing the folly of the rich, make allowance for their poverty in sense when compared with their own.

Cease from speaking vanity and using smooth speech; and excite not thyself at the forward and crooked. Yet how good is it for man to have his tongue smooth, when he cometh to seek understanding and wisdom!

Men of intelligence and understanding give five as the number of points from which knowledge and wisdom start, namely, Silence, Attention, Memory, Exercise, and Study; these form, as it were, the tower and wall of the edifice.

There are three things which distinguish a man, and without the full possession of which no one can be called - **Wise of heart**. They are as follows - Never to despise the man below thee in knowledge while he be earnest in acquiring learning; never to be jealous of the man who can command a richer home and a wealth of golden treasure; and never to ask payment of one whose heart is fully turned to the search after wisdom and knowledge.

In enquiring for knowledge, ask questions, even though they give evidence of folly; but in keeping knowledge, guard it as thou wouldst guard the diamond, agate, or amethyst.

He who is clothed in the garb of bashfulness while seeking wisdom, will on the morrow wrap himself in the cloak of folly; therefore, rend this garment, and take thy stand at the door of the wise, as the pauper at the door of the rich.

If a believer hath lost some form of knowledge, let him seek it at the hand of whomsoever it be yea, even at the hand of the sceptic it is right that its loss be restored.

To seek knowledge and search out wisdom, travel every city and spot; for what may be regarded as of little account by some may be considered of value by others.

Impart thy knowledge to him that knoweth not, and learn that of which thou art ignorant, and which thou dost not know; by doing so, thou wilt keep up afresh the knowledge which thou hast, and wilt continue to acquire information and learning anew.

Knowledge impressed upon the heart of the young is like engraving on stone, but if man take to learning in old age, it is like making an impression on sand.

Do not that violence to knowledge to place it in the hands of men who are the fools of society, lest thou commit a sin thereby; but put it in the hands of those who love its ways, and then life and grace thou shalt find.

As for the wise of heart, poverty will never debase him, nor will lust lead him astray; his knowledge is like unto a crown placed upon his head, and it draweth him along the path of right. Take heed thou observe that which thou hast been commanded, even though it be weariness to the flesh; furthermore, deal not with the wicked according to his deeds, lest thy reward from God be lost.

Beware lest thou condemn the boor who disputeth thy contention, when thou knowest his folly and senselessness; rather lay up thy wisdom for the man of understanding; for had the former been of the wise and understanding, he would have found delight in thy words.

Verily, knowledge which is not published is as a treasure buried in the dust of the earth.

Wisdom without action theory without practice hath its seat in the mouth; but by means of action, it becometh fixed in the heart.

The man who, in spite of the knowledge he hath and the hidden things made clear, transgresseth the commands and precepts of that knowledge, is as a physician that taketh to his bed through sickness, and yet partaketh of food that is unfit for him.

A man of knowledge, who by his wisdom is of use to others, yet neglecteth himself, is as a spring that refresheth the thirsty, itself seething in mud, mire, and dirt.

Men may be grouped under four heads; consider them and take a lesson from them. There is the one who knoweth and is aware that he knoweth; he is wise of heart, learn thou from him. There is the one who knoweth, but he is not aware that he knoweth; speak to his heart comfortingly and remind him thereof. There is the one who knoweth not, and hath fear, because he knoweth not; have pity upon him, and give him information. But as regards him who knoweth not, yet thinketh that he knoweth - the simpleton, shun him, and keep him far off.

Say not, I know and understand with regard to some whatsoever, earning of which thou hast no knowledge whatsoever; guard thyself from thus falling into a snare and trap, lest thou be suspected of ignorance even in that which thou dost know.

When a fool sinneth, he throweth the guilt upon him whom his sin hath put to shame; the man of knowledge and understanding is satisfied to bear the burden of his guilt on his own head.

He who speaketh as though he were wise, while utterly devoid of all wisdom, may be compared in his folly to the ass of the mill; day by day it goeth round and round, yet moveth not from its circuit, as though it were stricken in the feet.

Should not thy heart feel faint when thou seest the learned falling into the snare of the simple, men of honour falling into disgrace, and wealthy ones becoming impoverished, having come down to the lowest depths?

As for him who reproveth others, however clever he may be, if his own actions are not straight, will not his reproof fall upon the hearts of his hearers like rain coming down upon a stone?

Attend to four things in person, and consider not thine own self too high, although thou mayest have one hundred servants at thy command. Attend thyself to thy guests; do the honours to scholars; show due respect to thy well-beloved parents; and look after matters connected with thy stables, even though thou mayest drive pairs and teams.

He who walketh in the company of the wise will himself be honoured, and called great and noble; and thus, he who joineth with the simple will be despised, and he who feedeth with the fool will be broken.

See Wisdom enthroned as a king, and Beauty as his lieutenant! Yosef's beauty it was which bound him in the prison-house; his wisdom it was that brought him into the presence of the king.

Beware of the simpleton who is religious, and the fool who is ceremonial, also of the scholar who is without scruple; their hope will indeed be lost for ever.

A wise man was once asked by the men of his time - Who is the Lord of the Universe, our Creator? He replied - It is forbidden to investigate such a matter; we are too weak in our natures and would come to sin in the attempt to fathom it.

Knowledge is as a tree producing goodly fruit; if good fruit be in it, all is in it; if this be not in it, what is in it?

The best of possessions is knowledge; purchase it for thyself from those who sell it [i.e. teachers]. He who hath this as a possession, what doth he lacks? If he lacks this, what doth he possesses?

The subject of study inscribes on thy heart and repeat it twice and thrice until thou dost know. Exceeding much study may weaken thy sense, and the intellect becloud. The lamp, when trimmed, will burn on anew; fed with too much oil, it will burn itself out. Choose Wisdom as thy portion, so that it may be for a standard o'er thy head.

Shekel HaKodesh

Rabbi

Yosef Kimchi

On Humility

Meekness of spirit is the halo of the wise; impudence is the sign of the fool.

If thou hear one speak insultingly concerning thee, pay no heed to him, nor regard him, lest thou hear more cruel things said about thee, and thou wouldst stumble and fall.

Do not reply to the insult of a fool, for whatsoever the insult, it is less vile than the one who uttereth it. Silence is the best reply, for by silence thou canst best forget it.

Choose three things for thyself, and through them thou shalt find favour with the Creator of all - Humility, wherewith to subdue all folly; Reverence, by which to lessen sin; and Knowledge, teaching how to use moral suasion with men by the art of well-chosen language.

In mixing with men, it is often useful to be dumb,

though able to speak; to be deaf, though able to hear; and blind, though able to see. In this way thou shalt be much courted and become their chief and ruler.

He is not of highest quality who only abstaineth from harming his fellowmen, but he who taketh upon himself a share of the burden of their injuries; and whatsoever may happen, he goeth forth to meet them with a cheerful countenance.

The disciple of a Sage, once seeing his Master insulted by a fool, was incensed, and in his anger sought permission to handle roughly and to inflict bodily harm upon the offender; whereupon the Sage replied - Tis not the part of the wise to permit loss or bodily ill to be done to one's fellow-man.

The man who hath both much knowledge and humility, is called blessed by all who look upon him; for by the two he lesseneth the number of his foes, and his band of supporters increaseth.

The Wise Man spake - I will lift up my soul [can swear] - That no fault will be found in me when my humility shall be weighed in the balance.

The end of all strife and contention is regret; but the end of humility is strength and possession.

If a man cannot control himself, how can he sway another man's soul?

When in enmity a man scoffeth at words spoken in praise of thee, leave friendship undisturbed till the morrow; forget the reproachful word for the day, and perchance thou wilt have changed a foe into a friend. Be ready betimes to bend the knee, and to incline thy frame; take heed that thou be not slothful therein. When, with their hand, men throw a stone at thee, stoop, then shalt thou cause them to miss their aim, and thus thou shalt escape.

To endure pain is to halve the pain; to try to thrust it off, is to increase it.

Having had thy full say in reproach of another, bear him no further grudge; leave room for reconciliation. Seek no ruling position in thy city, and never look down upon thy inferiors.

O man, if one would honour thee by flattering words and false, strive thou until they may be applied to thee in all truthfulness. Trust no man who doth ascribe to thee deeds of merit which thou hast not performed. And if thy fellow men praise thee for some pre-eminence which is not in thee, turn thou from their company.

Be lowly and humble in spirit amid the greatness of thy glory; and have no care for the fortune which hath never come to thy hands.

When a man discerneth in others some advantage which he hath not, then is the time to regulate the sense of humility within him. If, for example, he sees one richer than he is, let him think that the other is a great man, and superior to himself in righteousness. If he observes a poor man, let him reflect that he is poor and lowly, and that his opportunities for sin are, therefore, poorer and less. If he beholds an aged man, one full of years, let him say - Truly his length of days are due to his devotion unto Heaven. When he looketh at a youth, let him realise that his transgressions have been few, and that his guilt is slight. If he sees one who is better informed, let him consider that he is pure and innocent in his intelligence. And if he regards the simple-minded, let him think, peradventure he will be judged for his sins in the balance which will weigh them but as errors of judgment.

To the way of humility, I incline, and thus my heart will be understanding gain.

Shekel HaKodesh

Rabbi

Yosef Kimchi

On Abstinence

To be too fond of this world and of that which is therein, provoketh the wrath of Heaven. If thou sacrifice this fondness, thou shalt be sure of the glory and grace of thy God.

All man's striving in this world is but for honour, riches, and ease; and yet he who loveth this life too much is often far removed from them, and more closely bound to sorrow and sighing.

Fret not for the store laid up, for the riches heaped of yore, fearing lest men rob thee of them, when they steal thy substance and wealth.

Leave that which thou requirest not, seize but that which thou dost need; then shall the glory of God be thy rereward, and good fortune shall be thy meed.

In the day of happiness, think of sorrow, and in the day of evil, hope in God, that He may deliver thee from the oppression of anguish and sickness.

See the advantage of poverty over riches! Be wise and feel thyself abashed and ashamed; for no man rebels against God's Word in attempting to get poor, but he doth so in the endeavour to grow rich.

Say unto the man who hath much provision - Have sufficient years been granted thee wherein to spend thy hoard?

Enquire of the man who hath gotten himself wealth, if he hath also assured himself of the years of his life. There are four causes of sorrow which affect men in this world - When poverty cannot extricate itself, so as to become strong by reason of wealth; when occupation leaveth no time for leisure, and is ever engaging a man; when there is no end to a man's longing for a thing which he can never obtain; and when there is unceasing care, which goeth on to the very end and finish.

A man of understanding who esteemeth himself will think little of this world's splendour.

Man in this world may be likened to the fruit of a tree; whilst ripening, it is gathered by those who find it; when matured, it is longed for and enjoyed by thsoe who see it; while if it be not gathered, it falleth, and the beasts trample it underfoot.

In the days of youth fear the day of death and depart from sin; for upon old camels the skins of young sheep are borne. When the lambs and the rams are in grazing, many of the young ones perish, and so on the shoulders of the old are the caskets of many young lives carried to the grave.

When a mortal passeth from this world, men of worth will ask, What life did he lead? But they who only think of earth enquire; How much did he bequeath to his children?

Is not man in this world, by accident and birth, as a creature e'er surrounded by serpents at every turn? Where'er he goeth, whene'er he cometh, they endanger his every path; in constant fear, he dreadeth lest now, by this one or by that, he be suddenly attacked.

He who mortifieth himself, ever thinking with delight of his latter end, will preserve his life unto eternity; while if he keepeth it alive for the pleasure of this world alone, let him know and understand that in this way he killeth the life that is within him.

Have a care and weep for man's mortality and rejoice not at life's pleasantries!

Proclaim unto people day after day the message; there they sit in silence, they answer not, nor give ear.... But when the Day of Judgment cometh, they will perforce rise up and stand in the presence of their Maker, called upon to give account of their wrong doings.

The man whose sole delight is in this world, may be likened to a dog sucking bones; thinking that it is sucking blood from the bone, it sucketh the blood of its own lips.

The man who doteth on this life, and serveth not his God, will ever be the loser, though he thinks that he doth gain. Indeed, he will be stripped of all that he hath done in the day when he doth change his garb, and putteth other raiment on.

When thou dwellest upon this thy world, think that thou wilt live for aye; when thou thinkest of this life's end, think that to-morrow it may slip from thee.

Righteousness is, in truth, the health of the soul; wickedness is its death.
Whosoever pineth at his fortune in life showeth he is angry with his Maker who formed him.

The man who can laugh away a single care may be said to have had life's desire accomplished by Heaven.

The man who, though the world esteem him highly, thinketh very little of himself, is sure to be delivered and released from the grasp of that which harmeth and hindereth.

Pride thyself upon the gain which thou hast already obtained; have remorse for those things which thou hast wilfully neglected.

Leave all gain that diminisheth and ceaseth, and take thou hold of the kind that goeth on and increaseth.

Let man in life, while in health and at ease, recognise and know that the breach may come great as the sea; for how can man remain whole and strong, seeing that Death is ever hanging at his neck?

A Sage, on observing a man full of care, enquired of him thus - Why in such deep thought? If thou art concerned with earthly things, thou hast little to hope, for at death thou shalt be parted from them. But if thou art anxious concerning thy latter end, then I say, may God increase thy care!

If, in true wisdom, thou dost test the world in which thou livest, reflecting on it, proving it, and searching it, thou wilt indeed find it like unto an enemy, wearing the mask and cloak of a friend.

Shouldst thou not fear, O man forewarned, when, without due provision, thou settest forth for the distant country, and lacking all things, thou descendest into the pit of destruction - The place of trouble and affliction, doomed to stand before thy Creator on the Judgment Day, to answer for the transgression of precept and command?

Covet not the wealth of men and their possessions, filled as their vessels are through oppression and violence. How many men gather riches that goeth to their foes, even to the lovers of their wives!

He who his freewill offerings doth reduce, and giveth ever less in charity, is but gathering and collecting wealth to swell the treasures of another.

Fear lest thou heap up for thyself the sins and bequeath unto thy heirs the monies.

As for the worries and calamities which Time bringeth with it, and all the occurrences of life, regard thou them as dreams, and think of them as though they had never been but fail, thou not to prepare food for the soul and some provision for the spirit.

No man is sure of his livelihood, and he is therefore never free from concern.

If in all his days here pursuing vain toil, man doth not obtain his will and desire, how can he attain his will in that world for which he had no feeling, and after which he never did run?

The man who revealeth his blemish to all forgetteth the honour of his own soul; but he who turneth from the love of this world, may truly be said to glorify the spirit within him.

Let man but establish his secret things, and his Creator will regulate the things revealed. If he attends to his latter end, He on high will lengthen the years of his life.

He who would preserve his life should call to mind the hour of death; and while he be yet in his day, let him fear the coming of his night.

Shekel HaKodesh

Rabbi

Yosef Kimchi

On Modesty and Shame

The innocent and shamefaced ones are known by their demeanour - They are such as have a sense of shame even when none other is nearby.

Have consideration for the worth of thy judgment and thy learning, lest thy conscience rise and reproach thee. Carefully arrange thy stores and the abundance of thy treasure, so that thou mayest cheerfully dispense thy dues, even thy gifts.

Man's modesty may be seen in the union of meekness and knowledge, in his observance of the Law and the moral precept, in his methods of living, and in the patient endurance of the events and accidents that befall him in life.

It is the part of the modest man, who shaped his actions well, to conduct himself through life as is meet, never to do aught in secret that he would blush to do openly.

Man's modesty may be said to consist of his keeping aloof from sinfulness, so that at all times his garments be white, he labouring to provide of that which cometh into his hand for his own wants, and to bequeath thereof unto his children.

Modesty may take four forms - That of greeting a friend in sincerity, that of attaching him in affection, that of fulfilling his wish at all times according to one's power, and that of being ever delighted to deal charitably by him.

Modesty is a quality much to be desired; it may always be discerned on the face of him with liberal heart, whereas its opposite is such as to cause pain and sorrow to the heart of its possessor.

As for the man who putteth on the garment of modesty, his blemishes will, in truth, be covered up and concealed; but he who doth divest himself thereof will render those defects clear to the eye of man, so that they be called to mind; nay, more, such a one will gather around him as his associates none but the worthless scoffer and the low fellow.

Faithfulness and Modesty are two sisters, one bearing witness to the other; at all times joined, as the onion's peel, one ever embracing the other.

Conduct thyself always with Modesty and Shame in passing through the years of thy pilgrimage here and see thou the upright way.

Shekel HaKodesh

Rabbi

Yosef Kimchi

On Self Denial

God's Word to Mother-earth did come - Hearken to my voice. And He did promise to support her task, if men, as true and faithful servants of the God on high, would work the ground with diligence.

Who is the man of wisdom, that may rightly boast of wisdom? Tis he who, recognising the sinful thing, keepeth himself aloof from it.

The man of sense who enquireth, and seeketh to remain firm, will not rest until he doth dismiss his desire, and drive it wholly away from him.

O man of understanding! Be not confident until thy sense hath conquered thy desire. If o'er thy own desire thou canst not rule, how canst thou over others rule? No man can be accounted upright until his sinful soul's desires be looked upon by him as so many abominations, equally abhorred as the mouse and other unclean things.

Things prohibited may be classed under three different heads; give them thy attention, and thou wilt easily discern them. There are things which thy soul longeth after, which thou shouldst keep at arm's length; some things may be prohibited for which thou hast no desire, leave these alone; some things, too, are prohibited, which, even if allowed, would find man's soul recoil from them.

Happy the man who divorceth his desire for the glory of that which cometh not nor appeareth; for no man will regret having stifled, to the glory of God, the desire that assailed him!

As for the man who ruleth not over his desire, his end will be all evil and bitter; and, as though stung in the heel by the adder, will be what the day bringeth him forth, his pain growing greater and keener.

Shouldst, thou seek counsel, and not find the adviser in whom thou canst confide, then turn from that which thy desire doth prompt, lest for thyself thou spread destruction's net. Lo, thy desire for thy good sense doth lie in wait, when sense doth stop its ear and close its eye!

Were it not for three considerations, things would go all well with man, and his right-doing would be assured, namely the powerlessness of old age to impress its experiences; the stubbornness with which pride is decked; and the desire of man which cometh upon him and is not vanquished.

He who taketh the counsel of his heart's desire will in a brief moment destroy the joy of his heart; but he who rebelleth against the promptings of desire will receive due honour, and, rising above, will prove himself the victor, and be helped.

Strive not with a miser, who delighteth in keeping and holding back from thee his wealth; strive rather with thine own desire, fight against it, and scatter thy fierce passion.

Tis ever so; while counsel sleepeth, passion waketh, watching at all times and hours. If wise counsel be overcome, rising passion showeth its brazen front.

If in goodness the child his life begins, he will continue so until old age; he who in his youth doth sin, will remain a sinner unto death.

How long, O man, will thy heart yet slumber? When wilt thou wake from thy sleep? The world's battles leaving, strengthen thyself, and fight with thy desire the goodly fight.

But shouldst thou, too fond of the beauteous world, to

its pleasures give way, understand, to the great sorrow of thy heart, thy remorse will grow apace.

Passion and blindness to each other as a pair do cling, they are caught in each other's embrace; joined together to destroy the beauteous strength of manhood, they associate always, and never part.

Who Heaven's trials in cheerful spirit doth receive, will ever gain the joyousness that bringeth with its true restfulness; while he who frets at what the hour may bring, will ne'er from sighs and sorrowing be free.

Faith in all things doth stand high; Tis unique and foremost in quality. Where there is faith, there is enough of grace and wealth, of substance strong, and of service full.

Not in proportion to one's haste will one's food, nor daily ration, come; should it elude thy grasp and leave thee, seek it until thou find it again.

What a fool is he who God's judgment and ruling contemned! There is no cure for such folly as his. When his time comes, it will avail him naught to show a sad countenance, or to betray anger and annoyance.

I will place God before me, that my hope be not lost.

I will resolve in my heart to make my way firm.

Shekel HaKodesh

Rabbi

Yosef Kimchi

On Man's Confidence and Despair

Trust in God in all thy actions, and into His Hand commit thy work; be thou pleased at what cometh or goeth, so that restful may be thy home-tent.

If Destiny will that fortune smile upon thee, it will come to thee, though thou art far away; or if it be ills thou'rt destined to bear, thou canst not elude them, though thou be borne to the skies.

Let no man fret over things not come to his hand, nor brought within his reach; but let him rejoice in the portion which God hath graciously given unto him, and he will be at ease, quiet and restful.

Trust in God whilst thou livest in the world, and thou shalt give rest to thy soul, and keep it alive; for know, not always hath the raven its food, not always hath the lion its store.

If thou but hast the help of God, the dry wood of the

forest will bear thee fruit, until thou shalt say - **Enough** but if He Above be not with thee, then even the garden-trees will not bring forth, their fruit they will deny, until thou shalt ask - Where are they?

A wise man once, in quest of his suit, came regularly at dawn to the palace of his lord, and day by day at the entrance-door would watch early, so that the master could never avoid him. The master then wrote him to name his desire, whereupon he replied in the following strain:

O hearken, dear Sire.

From a twofold cause do I knock at thy gates.

Expectant I am, for I am in dire straits.

Sore is the heart, it burneth as coal.

When help doth not come to the craving soul.

I've waited till now my foes to disarm.

Of revengeful spite and envy inane.

If they see me turn back, they will do me more harm.

For they'll jeer and revile, if my quest be in vain.

Say, therefore - **Yes**, and something do, or utter the one word - **No**.

And so, my soul at rest shall be, and the worst I then shall know.

To him who doth beg, say - Do not beg; are not all things in the hands of God?

To beg of thee something I have come; from God, I have asked it first. If thou art willing my request to grant, my thanks both to God and to thee I will speak; but even then, my God I will thank, shouldst thou not fulfil my wish; and as for thee, while praise be denied, I will not judge thee ill.

When thou wouldst act, above thee look, and thine own failings learning, raise thou thyself in perfection's way; but in concerns of money, below thee look, and rejoicing, Him thou wilt praise, who giveth thee thy daily bread.

He who in the Rock, his Maker, trusteth, will be lifted on high; he will not look on his calamity; from ills safe delivered he will be.

Shekel HaKodesh

Rabbi

Yosef Kimchi

On Deliberation and Endurance

Deliberation, when occasion calls, is worth four hundred zuz.

Wait, and thou shalt thyself deliver, as the hart and the fowl from the snare; hasten, and unto thy soul thou wilt bring care and worry.

To deliberate with good effect will expedite affairs; while undue haste, with bad result, like shafts in the heart of man doth act.

Choose for thyself the longer way, for its portion is set in a pleasant place; eschew the path that shorter seems, it leadeth oft to sorrow and pain.

The man who is in haste to do a thing will fail in strength and power; wisely hesitate, then act, and thou'lt more quickly gain thine end.

Endure the truth though it be bitter, and thou shalt be called a patient man; growl not at that which thou dost suffer and throw not the blame upon the world.

Is not endurance of two kinds, the endurance which will bear the stress and storm of evil times, and the endurance which suffereth hurt in souls inured to sinfulness from days of long ago?

Think of God whene'er thy baser nature would prevail, then shalt thou from all danger be redeemed; but should the world against thee set its face, remember, hail the power of patience at every turn.
 At good prepare to offer thanks and praise, nor less at every ill; a sickness sore, a grievous malady, is the sorrowing of heart for that which hath not come.

Better than sorrow is of poison the draught, for care is locked in man's heart; according to his height, his fall doth come; the course that his descent will take doth mark his former strength and might.

Conquer thy mourning by the power of endurance, lest thy sorrow be prolonged for ever; choose unto thyself the counsel of sense, and securely thou shalt pass thy days and thy years.

Misfortune that's conquered will oft-times prove a blessing in disguise; endure then, and bear what thou canst not escape, and quiet thou shalt be, from sin delivered, and free from all guilt.

To attain his desire by bearing ills, the power to mortal is given, for no man is free like unto them that endure; therefore, O man, but endure, and trust in the mercy of Heaven.

Understand, there is no nobler thing, and nothing more discreet, than to acknowledge a kindness with thanks, and to meet misfortune with a heart all brave. Let every man of sense confess that all things come from God.

Shekel HaKodesh

Rabbi

Yosef Kimchi

On Sufficiency

He who with little is well content is rich indeed as a king; and a king, in his greatness, is poor as the pedlar, when his kingdom sufficeth him not.

He whom God's gifts do suffice is rich enough in store; while he who is rich and hath a store, yet nothing that he gets him sates, is poor, indeed, for he's distressed.

Be content with that which God to thee hath given and look not at another's lot; find thy delight in Him, and when thou dost ask, He will grant thee thy request.

How, little food sufficeth man! A man will eat and leave thereof. Happy the man who hath no greed, craving but his daily bread! As for the jealous man of lust, the world his wants cannot supply.

If small as is thy wont, thy ration cometh not to thee,

seize upon the little, by thine own efforts gained, rather than be put to shame and humbled before men; let thy trust be ever in thy God.

Take of that which is prepared enough to keep thee from want and harm and scorn the royal crust; for all thy glory vanisheth, fading as the grass; as suddenly and quickly as it cometh, so quickly doth it go.

A little will keep thee from disgrace and contempt; this little will therefore be better and sweeter than the glamour and mammon, the wealth and great store, that are likely to lead thee to shame and derision.

Prize not too dearly thy neighbour's great substance and wealth; nor let the little lot, found in thine own dwelling, be despised of thee.

Order well thy supplies, for by methodical outlay they go twice as far; but without regulation, as a vineyard without fence, half thy food will go to others, and but one half will remain to thee.

Be wise, and think not less of the pence; so, show not thy full power to the poor in strength. Glory is like the high mountain dust; the beauteous sceptre is lost in an hour.

If two foes there be that ne'er join and unite, they are

known as contentment and greed; if rest thou wouldst have in the blending of work, choose the former, and thy work will prevaile.

Ye versed in the sciences, ancient and new, having searched and enquired, tell me now - Is there a joy that resembles the joy of the heart? Can any wealth equal the wealth of the soul?

Should fortune upon thee not smile, let thy heart be trusty and stayed; remember the hardships and trials, the hard things now past, and thou shalt find rest and repose.

If thou seekest not more for thyself than is good, thou wilt learn to be content with thy ration of food.

Renounce the thought of another man's wealth, then honour and glory are thine. In renouncing alone there is freedom, better than all things; Tis better than all merchandise, for by it thou gainest the truth.

There is no sin greater than greed without measure; be girded and bridle thy soul from desiring. If the loss of a friend thou bewail without measure, e'en thy faith will in time be found to be waning.

Ever rejoice in thy portion, be content with a morsel of food, and with trembling cling to God and His fear.

Shekel HaKodesh

Rabbi

Yosef Kimchi

On Kindness and Charity

He who doth choose charity for a fortress will find men of their own accord humble themselves before him; against all daily accidents and dire calamity, there's naught to shield a man like deeds of kindness. A two-fold debt thy neighbour doth claim, observe it, inscribe it on thy heart; all kindness deal, all ill withhold, lest soon he strives with thee.

A two-fold debt thy kinsman doth claim; let this be thy constant rule; though he refuses to give to thee, give thou to him; though he keeps far away from thee, be thou ever at his side.

If thou wilt but reflect that all thy sustenance is given by the grace of God and His mercy, thou wilt come to see that Heaven hath placed in thy hands the poor man's dues, even the food of him who lacketh all things.

He who pitieth not his kith and kin, yet giveth of his

wealth to strangers, is like unto her who giveth suck unto her neighbour's child, while her own doth pine from starvation and want.

He who much wealth and riches doth gather by means not just and right, is like unto him who thinketh that without pegs and cords his tent will stand erect and firm.

The man who giveth not according to his wealth, but is close-fisted and mean, will, by Heaven's decree, lose power over his wealth, for it will go to the rulers on earth.

Tis hard to rise and win the heights, but easy is the fall; just like this stone, though large, it will easily roll down, but hard it is to raise it.

As the spirited horse, though famished and worn, keepeth straight to his course, and falleth not by the way, even so is the generous of heart with his gifts; another to stay, he'll go foodless himself.

Tis not for wealth, but for name and fame, that the liberal of heart do care; but the miser will tarnish his honour and name in trying to save his glittering treasure.

Though fortune smile upon thee now, thou canst not

tell if she will turn to thee another time.

The generous will promise, and promptly pay, before men for payment apply; but the miser delayeth his vow to pay, perchance some pretext may come forth by the morrow.

Shouldst thou be asked to promise a thing, and thou art afraid and feareth regret, rather say - **No** than yield with a - **Yea**, for by giving it not, thou wouldst stumble and sin.

When thou has said - **Yes**, to a thing bear it, and fulfil thy word; for having said - **Yes**, it is to thy shame to say - **No**, and thus abstaining, to break thy word.

Deal kindly while the breath of life is within thee, ere hither and thither thou flittest, and thy righteousness goeth before thee.

Shekel HaKodesh

Rabbi

Yosef Kimchi

On Poverty and Asking Help

Woe to the man who loseth his riches and pleasures together, while all that remaineth to him are the same habits and methods.

If thou dost give to a man, thou wilt become his lord and master; be not dependent on a man, and then thou shalt be on the same level with him.

The respect which thou payest to a man will come back to thee again in return; be beholden to a man when thou art in need, and by him thou wilt be lightly esteemed.

This is poverty indeed, and as a snare that is spread for thee, when thy heart is ne'er free from the dread of poverty.

If even thy request thou dost obtain, think not in thy heart that relief thou hast found; for if, by asking, thou hast lightly thy honour esteemed, thy loss will be greater than thy gain.

Of all the bitter things thou hast tasted, is there one more bitter than to beg a favour from thy friends and companions?

Rather endure want than beg a favour from one unaccustomed to give; for the worst part of asking is felt at the time when thou takest the gift with a blush. Better by far to encounter a bear than to encounter a fool; but in meeting the man with a liberal heart, tranquillity of soul shall be thine. For while he doth give to another his dole, the liberal man himself doth feel the shame of the other, his language and tone are delicious; the kindnesses done thee he ne'er will recall, to oblivion they all are consigned.

He who asketh for more than he doth require or more than is his wont, will find his just reward in this - He'll be denied and suffer want.

The man who putteth off the date of his giving, on whose word thou canst never rely, may be likened to a figure painted and copied, the mere image and form of the real.

If thou goest to a miser to ask a favour, he will surely refuse thee and be also thy foe; if he meets thee abroad, or meet thee at home, not a word will he give thee, not even a glance.

To be the guest of a miser is to suffer want that cannot be described; his horse will go fasting, left without fodder; and so, will the guest, not receiving that which he doth require.

How ill a thing is poverty! Niggardliness is worse. The man who turneth to the miser bringeth upon himself contempt and shame.

Tis better for a man to be carried to the grave than to beg a gift from the miser; for he'll be like the fisherman who goeth forth, thinking to catch fish in a desert of sand.

A kind-hearted man once said to his friends, let this secret arrangement be binding upon us; Never beg a favour of me but through a trusty friend, or by letter; for if thou dost ask it with thy lips, two-fold will be the loss; your dignity will suffer, and all my merit will be gone.

Shouldst, thou need a gift, ask rather of one who once was rich and hath become poor, than ask of one who was once poor and hath now become rich, and is a man of means.

Only then from the miser shouldst thou take a gift, when from the generous thou gettest no help. Surely the lion will not turn from feeding on curs, if he finds no sheep his hunger to still.

Thy townsmen all will shrink from thee, if thy hearth be enclosed and narrow; but if no bars keep thee back, and so prevent thy going forth, then on thy way thou shalt not find the thorns to vex thy path.

And like to myrrh are waters pure which run along the ground; the freshness, aye, the scent thereof, is wafted in man's face; but standing water stagnant turns, its odour doth affect the nostril most unpleasantly.

Tis in the hour when thy worldly goods are few, that thou must beware that thou be not poor in spirit and soul.

Shekel HaKodesh

Rabbi

Yosef Kimchi

On Silence and Speaking Opportunely

Silence is never the loser; in speaking there's always regret; Tis far better to be silent and still, than to babble and be nearer to sin.

Thy words and acts are in thy power before the word is spoken; once said, the word hath power over thee, all control from thee hath passed.

Why speak of something which, when known, will do thee harm, and bring about thy fall? If not spoken and made known, thou still hast hope that it may accrue to thy profit.

The penalty of silence is less than that of speech. Who can tell how bitter, and sore may be the pain of speech?

Bind the tongue fast, and let it not loose, lest thou bring on thy head much guilt; if silence doth bring one remorse and regret, how endless the train that speaking will bear.

Thy tongue binds fast, as thou wouldst a treasure bind; for if thou heed not, it will fare ill with thy soul.

If thou wouldst choose the right and proper counsel, then choose the muzzle for thy mouth, and silence for thy lips.

Within the mouth of man his stumbling block doth lie; as a thief it lieth in wait under his very tongue; at its bidding man falleth low, bearing punishment at every turn; and thus, indeed, he doth increase his sorrow manifold.

O creature, see how He who in the heaven dwelleth created thee! Two ears and eyes thou hast, two cheeks and feet; two knees and hands thou hast, two loins and thighs, yet a single tongue in an enclosure hid, but two tongues never. Two walls, moreover, He hath designed, they are the lips and teeth. Doubly cautious be then with thy words, closely thy tongue to heed, and an asset it will be to thee to safeguard thee for life.

In man's mouth lieth length of days, life and death are between his cheeks.

How goodly if man's sense doth rule the words that

from his lips do flow! But when his words his sense do rule, they become his chiefest foe, his bitterest enemy.

If thou cease from speaking, respect for thee will grow; and likewise, thy reverence will fail by the multitude of words.

Tis good if speech can remove some harm or be of use to thee; where its is not - Twere better far to hold thy peace; speech hath no hope for thee.

If idle words one's sense outrun, their mastery over man is gained; but if in man his sense prevails, his words do all to him belong.

Let thy words be few, and thy faults will be few; increase thy words, and thy woes will increase.

If in the night thou wouldst wish within thine own dwelling to speak, take heed and lower thy voice, and softly utter thy words; or even in daytime listen well, and hear; nay, whilst thou art thinking, look round and see, if the matter which thou hast in mind may safely be spoken aloud.

A slip of the tongue may cost a man his head; he may by his own words be destroyed; whilst a slip of the foot, though sudden the hurt, may quickly be cured and restored.

O ye who would be wise, the root of things consider; set thy heart to understand them, and thou shalt find that under four heads they may all be classed; learn thou their secret and investigate them. Some things, at first, of service are, yet caution bid as they proceed; some things do neither harm nor good, these shun and best avoid; there are things, too, where danger lurks both at the start and finish; and there are things which are all good both at the end and the beginning. Then leave the three that go before, and the fourth head seize, hold fast.

At all times keep this rule in mind - there's something still better than silence; Tis this - to speak the truth.

The word of the wise will turns away anger and wrath, and many a word will restrain the revengeful spirit.

The wise-hearted one, in speaking, will often relieve, by refraining from speaking, he will doubly redeem. His words to the lowly bringeth relief; they are addressed to the haughty, when they spread out their nets.

If a man be not an expert in his work, let him not speak with too great confidence on that matter.

Nothing is of greater honour to a man than the word fitly and rightly spoken; it setteth a golden crown upon his head, and placeth the chain of gold around his neck.

To speak what is folly, yet know how to get clear by thy speech, is better by far than not to speak at all. Much better to appear as a sluggard, when called on to do something deceitful and false, than to hasten and join in the attempt, and suffer thyself to be broken.

Before all things guard thy mouth, and then as the hart from the hand of the huntsman thou shalt be delivered.

Shekel HaKodesh

Rabbi

Yosef Kimchi

On Truth

The wise find relief in truth and equity, fools in laying hold of lying and conspiracy.

When one young in years once rose up, and an old man opposing, endeavoured to speak, they addressed him and said - Shame on you! Hold your tongue! How dare you stand up to oppose such a man, whose years are such as to claim our submission? Whereupon he replied - Knowest thou not that Truth is much greater and older than he?

Answer the wise in a fair, honest way when they discuss a matter with knowledge and wisdom; give ear to such, and they will become thy benefactors, for truth is a thing to be loved, desired, and received with favour; and even though our friend be a Plato, great and exalted, and renowned for his learning, the right of our judgment we claim in the matter of truth, for Truth is to us a friend dearer by far than aught.

Speak the truth without favour, and respect not old age; Truth is older, strong in years as the world.

Knowledge is slighted, unsupported by wealth; whilst wealth without knowledge hideth many a stain. The rich man, though he lieth, is justified by wealth; the poor, though speaking the truth, seek justice in vain.

To me it seems strange that men should expend such marvellous wealth and fabulous sums on the purchase of knaves to serve them as slaves, since they might easily gain, without price or pain, the hearts of the free by mere courtesy, by one pleasant act, and speech full of tact.

The wealth that's gained from vain pursuits decreaseth; whilst he who setteth his hand to save, gradually increaseth. To speak the truth be thy resolution bold.

Shekel HaKodesh

Rabbi

Yosef Kimchi

On Companionship and Association

Above all, thy true and faithful companion thou shouldst know, his faults to pardon and to forgive his sins; the man who is ever ready to seek offence, keep at arm's length, let him meet his own kind.

Experience will teach thee that good more or less lurketh in everything, save in the attachment of fools; be it, there-fore, thy rule to avoid them altogether.

Adopt the advice honestly given to thee which agreeth with thine own common sense; but reject the counsel that is approved by thine own base desire.

Choose an associate who will always be thine, and ready to serve thee as thine own hand, bending before thee in all things, as though a true slave all in thy power.

Take heed to pay to thy companion's true regard, so that they be bound as friends, closely attached to thee;

bestow on them all thought and heart, when they make their call, provide for them a proper place, a cosy seat, and comfort during their stay; and while they speak, open thou thy ears to catch their every word.

Two couples are closely attached, like threads in the weaver's loom; they are Silence, the sister of Goodwill, and the Darer, who to the Doer is kin [lit., and the Tempter, who is brother to the Murderer].

Change not a friend that is old and dear for a new, while the old one is heart and heart with thee still. Contemn not a man because he doth err. Let not one man be despised of thee; in like manner, a thousand friends will never suffice; let thy substance and silver win them for thee.

The substance and the wealth of man, though wingless, fly away; but correction is a treasure true; there is no fortress like a friend.

Choose a comrade in whom thy heart believeth; for a man who hath not such a friend, is as the left hand without the right.

Choose among men the comrade in whom thy heart can safely trust; throw off the brother who, with deceitful heart, doth build the traitor's home, though he washes it white and clean.

If only by the flesh we go, among kinsmen near we claim a brother; but if we think of soul and spirit, we call our friend our kith and kin.

When with men thou wouldst mix, choose him who will not lead thee astray, so as to cause thee to stumble and fall; And all through life with this one aim, a man will suffer to serve his friend; and when he finds him sorely tried, he'll labour hard to set him free.

Be thou ready and first thy companion to greet, and to give him warm welcome and an honourable place; and when thou dost call him, and wish to address him, be sure that thou call him by his dear pet's name.

There is no greater boor on earth than he who, looking out for all men's errors, attacheth blame to them, while he doeth just the very same; and while he his own defects doth hide, and will not see his faults, he looketh round and findeth fault with all that others do. Companions may, in truth, be classed in threefold groups - attend to these, and thou soon wilt learn the mystery. Some comrades act as food to men, thy endless joys depend on them; the boast and worth of others seem like drugs, for certain times prescribed; there are those, too, who, like recurring sickness lurk, and bring naught but endless harm to health.

To join with fine natures is a source of great pride; to join with the senseless bringeth pain and remorse.

Choose him for thy friend who will always be thy pride, who, when aught thou dost want, will be ready to help thee; or, when thou dost utter what is in thy mind, in him thou shalt find a champion bold; or, should it e'en fare thy temper thou lose, he'll bear with thy words at all times and all seasons.

He may be called a fast friend and true who, with all his strength and might, will raise thee on high.

The friendship of a stupid man is bound to end in sorrow; a wise man will find relief and refreshing if he holds aloof from him

The best of beasts requires the whip; the best of wives their lord and sire; the wisest man advice doth need, without it will his wisdom lack.

Between thy two selves thy friend to task do call; and if thy reasoning he will not heed, then tax him further in the presence of a third. If he takes the caution, regard him as a gain; but if he yield not, think him wanting in sense; he will scarcely be missed when his number is called.

Reprove not, and waste not your words on a man; for

if his own sense upbraid not, how can another reprove?

How good it is to mix with men who know their worth and station! Turn far from him who's not of these; in his friendship there is no blessing.

The friendship that is perfect is always free from feud and strife; the truest sign of friendship is two hearts made one for ever.

Always join and never part from the man of fine spirit and unruffled mind; in his attachment and friendship thou thyself shalt be courted, and in the face of all men thou shalt be acknowledged.

Esteem the friend who chideth thee at any time, but not in the presence of another; and let him think he hath gained thereby some part at least of thy power and possession.

Plant the love of thy friend in thy very life's soil, as thou wouldst labour to fasten the pegs to thy tent; and if thou wilt plant, it with liberal root, it will be borne on the tongue, as fruit on the branches are borne.

The eye of a needle is not too narrow to hold two friends that agree; the breadth of the world is not sufficiently wide to contain in its fold two foes.

Dost, thou wish to prove thy friend, to know if he be false or true, ask thine own heart to act as diviner, and the truth it will surely divine.

Trust not the man who boreth thee with his troubles, but keepeth from thee his joys; his tongue may be all smooth for thee; his friendships but alloy.

Love thou the man who first hath done thee good, and return him help and kindness; so, love the man thou hast gained as friend, for in his heart thy friendly acts all friendliness do blend.

Love thy friend more than thou wouldst thy brother; for until he becometh my truest friend, how can I love even a brother?

Hid deep in the heart true friendship is found, its impression is sealed on the tongue; men's hearts are as mirrors that see eye to eye, their secrets are never revealed.

Play not the hypocrite with thy friend, nor by questioning people pry into his secrets, lest thou meet with a man who will blacken his name, and so estrange from thee his friendship.

Deal freely with thy friend with all thy wealth and very life; do likewise unto thy kinsmen with thy substance, mind, and speech; be courteous unto all men, and greet them on thy way; and as for thine enemy, be thou liberal and kind unto him, when he is sorely in need of thy charity and service.

Beware of the man who loveth thee when it suiteth the occasion, and serveth his purpose; for he will quickly turn his back when thou findest out his true aim and way.

Impart, as in winnowing, thy love to a friend, and never reveal the secret of another; when thine enemy cometh to make peace with thee, implore thou God on his behalf.

Put not thine hand to a thing if thou wilt not complete it, so that the reward be not lost. If thou once say - **Yes**, with regard to a matter, never change it to - **No**.

If thou find a companion whose thoughts thou art able to gauge, cleave unto him; for men's faults are beyond mortal ken; this one thou knowest thoroughly, then stand by him.

Like an earthenware vessel is the love of a fool; once it is broken, to its former condition it will never return; the friendship that is formed between men of discretion is like a vessel of gold, hard to break, and easily mended.

With the froward and haughty indeed it will go like an earthenware vessel, when knocked, it is broken beyond repair; but the man of good sense and discretion will be like glittering gold; he will brighten when beaten and be roused to do better.

Not at once, but by steps and degrees, disclose thy deep love for thy friend; as, not at once, but month by month, the tree bringeth forth its new fruit, so confess thy love by degrees, and fulfill thy friend's desire.

Beware of evil companionship, where nothing is wise or right; for by associating with the evil-disposed, thou wilt learn every bad habit and trait.

The man who can live with a woman of ill-heart showeth, indeed, what is patience, and more, what is skill; he resembleth the wolf of the forest, forsooth, which never changeth its nature, though it changeth its hair.

What wound or eruption is like unto her who leaveth her husband to lead her own life? In his heart she doth rankle as a bad, putrid sore; though sick of her, rid of her ne'er he can be. What disease can equal such suffering of soul, such affliction of heart, and grief without end?

In making thy choice, take thy seat with the best, and

thou shalt be honoured by God and by man; but if with the senseless thou chooseth to sit, thy comrades will lead thee to naught but disgrace.

Tis not good that man, though wise, should gain his end always. Tis not wealth that hath the power to hide one's guilt from view; where wisdom ruleth, man's faults and crimes may soon be blotted out of sight. Let silence as a muzzle to thy mouth be e'er applied; and see, too, that thy words are few, and cautiously restrained. If knowing this, thou dost not heed this sage advice - Tis better far thy bones should perish in the grave.

The man who rusheth in where his honour and fame are at stake, dare not quarrel with the world, if they suspect him of evil intent.

There are four things which lead men on to strife and ruin dire - haughtiness, and stubbornness, indolence, and rashness of desire.

The companionship of a foolish man is as a tooth that giveth pain; for both there is but one and the same cure - pluck it out. Thou canst not long endure his wicked senseless talk; for soon, indeed, without delay, thy love will turn to hate.

Change not the charms which grace thy wife for

another woman's charms - For, leading thy good sense astray, lust means to play thee false. A wiser man than thou once fell, King Solomon was his name; then see that thou art truly wise and fall not in sin's way.

Of all choice things a friend do choose; seek his wishes to fulfil, however great the task, and thus his friendship set upon thy heart.

Shekel HaKodesh

Rabbi

Yosef Kimchi

On the Testing of Friends, their Indulgence, and Forgiveness

A faithful friend him thou shouldst call, who cheerfully renders thee help; whether money or life is what is required, he is ready to meet thy need.

If thou wouldst select a friend worthy the name, try him, and see, if he'll stand this one test - If, when thou dost cross him and thwart him, he will keep true as before, he is the man thou shouldst hold, for he loveth thee no less.

Trust not him who praiseth thee when he be in want, and awaiteth thy help; but trust him who speaketh of thee with pride, even when thou refusest his request. Three things prove if men are wise; learn them well, and never shalt thou turn to folly - Be humble amid all provocation; be a hero in the fight; be pleased to grant a man's request.

If lovingly thou do a thing, thy former faults will be

concealed; if sullenly thou show thyself, thy secret sins will be disclosed.

Think not ill of any man, if once thy pardon he hath craved; forgive and pardon all his guilt, if once his sin he hath confessed.

As for him who will not trust the apology sincerely made, nor readily forgive the man who hath frankly said - I've erred, deem his friendship as though it had never been, and give him now a good wide berth.

When, for their guilt or shortcomings, thy friends beg indulgence, forgive; for know, forgiveness is in the heart of generous men; it's in the path of intelligence. Judge all men's errors kindly, even before thy indulgence is craved; nor think ill of the man whose guilt is not proved, for in this case the guilt will be thine.

From the day of a man's apology, harbour not in thy mind his wrongdoings, though his wrong may be clear, and he may offer a doubtful excuse; understand thou this and be not unkind.

No man can be found more neglectful than he who doth not choose the most genial of friends; yet far more neglectful is he, the prodigal, who, once having made them, loseth the friends he hath won.

Receive the man who, be he true or false, cometh to thee with regret for past offence; for, in this very act of his humiliation, he raiseth thee in men's esteem.

When a man refuseth in public to obey thee, he showeth that thou hast some honour to lose; and whenever in private he offereth thee slight, doth he not show that he feareth thy superior power?

Pardon transgression and sin in fools, as thou wouldst pardon them in nobler men.

Refuse not to give to a man, though he may have refused thee thy request; and refuse not to pardon, though he may have done thee harm.

To confess thy sin is thy very first task, when forgiveness for trespass thou seekest; for should thy denial confession preclude, thou hast nothing further to hope, as thy sin will be graver, aye, double.

Be quick to pardon thy friend's transgression; and should he become thy foe, reveal it not in the course of thy contention.

Have control over men and thou wilt find thy delight; be revengeful, and thou wilt find care and woe.

Before some deed thou wouldst perform, consider

well, hast thou the power to do it? If, say, thou givest order that a man be killed, hast thou the power to dispose of him; thus, or is thy command empty as the wind, which goeth forth only to return whence it came?

Why should a man who sinneth all his days, when his fellow committeth one sin against him, fly into a rage, and forget that his own trespass and sin are not by the world forgotten?

If, in the multitude of words, thou speakest against thy friends, let it not seem hard to thee, if they speak against thee also.

Pardon the man who hath sinned and confessed, pardon him in full, and forgive him completely.

Shekel HaKodesh

Rabbi

Yosef Kimchi

On Discernment and Manners

Not in the warning by experience bought, doth highest wisdom lie; but to be forewarned, and not to fall, this is true wisdom.

The man of understanding who hath his heart directed well, discerneth that which is far from right, and keepeth himself therefrom; and knowing, though regretfully, in what his strength is weak, he resteth content, and moveth not beyond the limits of his power.

No man's faith can be secure, whose perception is not sure; he will not open his mouth to speak, if he doth not understand the trend.

Abide thy opportunity and keep thy tongue on guard; give attention to thy subject and consider well thy task.

In a clever man's writing and talk thou wilt see a proof

of his faculties, of his spirit and mind; so also, a gift, and the way the gift comes, will show a man's nature, his motive, and thought.

Take care of the good things found in creation; beware of the evil and bad.

In truth, man's body and soul have taints in them both; why expect, then, that either be perfect or whole?

Wouldst thou o'er people rule with delight, deal with them kindly, and not with brute force; if respect and all honour thou wouldst from them win, then see that thou fail not their love to obtain. If thou but draw their hearts with a thin silken cord, their bodies and chattels thou'lt gain without fail.

As long as thou rulest with decency and ease, thou wilt sway the good folk, the best among men; at thy word of command, they'll encamp or move on; but if thou wouldst know how with the baser and rougher to act, I say, thou wilt only subdue them by keeping them under the heel.

Before I can gauge another man's worth, it behoves me to know my own backbone and strength, and to conduct myself towards men with a kindness that alone is able to win.

Shekel HaKodesh

Rabbi

Yosef Kimchi

On Keeping a Secret

Divulge not to thy friend a secret, the secret which thou wouldst conceal from thy foe. When thy friend revealeth a secret unto thee, forget it, and dismiss it from thy mind.

When men reveal unto thee a secret, keep thou dark the relation and also the author.

If thy friend doth transmit a secret by letter, and deemeth thee worthy of his confidence, then destroy the epistle, as though it had never been seen by thee; forget it, and let it depart from thy heart.

When a man tells thee his secret, hide both the secret and him that tells it; hide it as a treasure-trove, and let thy heart for ever be its grave.

When a man reveals a matter, and lay bare a secret, how can he be trusted with silver and gold?

If thou entrust thy secret to another, and he feel in his judgment that he cannot but disclose it, then do not attach to thy friend all the blame, thy own heart was not wide enough to contain it.

If a man's heart be too narrow to keep a secret, but it burneth like a fire in the range, it boots not to guard his mouth with a muzzle, for his tongue and his lips cannot be barred.

A secret not told is thine as a prisoner for ever; once told to thy friend, thou art its prisoner, and thou mayest fall. When thou tellest a hidden secret to another, see that thou make the right choice; for it should never be told unto two; it is for thee to judge who is the one.

A secret between two is locked in the heart; the secret of three is one cried in the street.

Why blame a man for unfolding thy secret, if thine own heart was distressed in keeping it hid? If thou thyself thy secret cannot conceal, why expect another to keep it, seeing that the thing is not his?

Of him who from a friend a secret doth bear to a third, it may be said that from the right path he hath turned; keep, therefore, thy mouth as with a bridle.

Shekel HaKodesh

Rabbi

Yosef Kimchi

On Kingship

Tis sad for a man when the king is his plaintiff and foe; for soon his own land will renounce him. God thou shouldst fear, as it behoveth His greatness; and cling to the king, his voice to obey.

Know that as one are the king and the law, as brothers on guard at every watch; one without the other can never stand firm; one without the other will never endure.

Live in a town where there is a king that is feared, where there's a judge that is all-just, and where the waters of the stream never fail; where a market is open, and their dwells one wise in all lore, one to heal all thy ills, an expert in his craft.

On one equal plane are the king and the fire; remove from them, and their help thou wilt need; approach them too closely, how soon with their heat they'll consume thee, if thou be not on thy guard.

If, in striving with thee, the king views thee askance, beware lest thou face him and turn to him straight; see, too, that thy words are remarkably few, or they will fail to gain for thee thy suit.

A king, through strict justice, doth establish the land, for his subjects by truth he doth lead; better is he than a season of plenty, and better than food and rich produce is the light of his countenance.

The worst kings are they who frighten the upright and good; they rule the worst who make offerings grow few; the worst of companions is he who misleadeth his friend; and so, the land full of plenty, which is not safe, is hateful to live in; it giveth no rest.

If a man oppresses his neighbour, to the King or Prince he'll appeal; but if the king act with rigour, and rob a man of his justice, to whom shall the man lift up his plaint and his cry, and whither shall he then turn for justice?

While the king is in anger stand not before him, for as a lion he will tear and seize on the prey; turn from the storm, and escape to the mountain; stand not by the stream while the waters overflow.

Strength and honour are a crown to the head of the wise man, who can boast of the king as his friend. If he be likened to the high hill and steep, where the cypress and nard their rich fragrance distill, let him remember there also do serpents dwell, they in their lurking place crouch; from thence, too, wild lions and leopards may leap. The ascent has been hard, indeed; but even now, thinking thou hast a firm footing, thou standest as though on the grave.

If the Regent doth hate thee, and sorely oppress thee, then trust not the love of the King; but the Regent as friend may turn the King's wrath and spare thee to walk securely.

Keep God's command, obey the King's word, and then in safety shalt thou go on thy way.

Shekel HaKodesh

Rabbi

Yosef Kimchi

On Stupidity, Pride, and Folly

Five faults may be found in a fool, and these cannot be found in any other - he showeth anger without any cause; mogivesf his labour is useless and vain; when he maketh a resolve to give aught away, not to the fit doth he give. nor his love nor his hate knoweth its bounds; and in time he betrayeth the secret that his friend hath not told.

How, little distinction doth the world draw between the fool and the upright and pure - Tis as the pearl of high price found in the desert, the value of which is not known.

Three things there are at which the heart groweth faint - When redoubled pains the wise attack; when madmen lead the man of sense; when the wicked hold sway over the righteous and good.

Six are ever victims of anxious care - the rich, who from his height hath fallen; the rich who, sooner or later, feareth a fall; the man that's revengeful and full of spite; the slave of ambition, whom nothing will sate; and he who seeketh for high honours, unsuited to his station.

If we weigh the hate of the wise and the love of the fool in the balance - I prefer to endure the hate of the wise, the prudent will say.

He who with a fool consorteth will himself become a fool; but he who with the wise of heart doth walk, will have a name like myrrh diffused, when crushed by human hand; just as the wind, driving across the fragrant spice, will bear to every face the sweet perfume, the beauteous scent. But should the wind o'er carrion pass, far different is the case; for smells, and stench, and odours ill, will sicken all the air.

Equal all and on one plane are friend and foe to the fool; what matters it, to whom all's the same? For his folly there is no cure.

What man is he who has to thank himself for bringing his shame to view? Tis he who entereth the place where folly hath no right; who will perforce his own seat choose, when once his seat's assigned; who talketh too much, and what is worse, talketh out of time.

When a fool has had his say, of his swearing take no note.

The man all meek, who cannot boast, will betimes receive a brother's help; but the high and haughty will be abased, and trampled in the dust.

He doth err who on his wit and counsel doth rely; he will surely fall, who trusteth to his sense alone.

I wonder why, O man of reason, thou settest not thy heart to think - Why be vain? Why proudly boast? Dost, thou forget thy origin - Nature's part in the begetting.

The man, in senseless pride bedecked, deems his own soul too dear; boasting his powers beyond all due, he congratulates himself; but from the time he thinks he is rising, he will be sure to find that he is being brought down low.

Be not led by a fool to tread into the heap and so bespatter thyself.

Shekel HaKodesh

Rabbi

Yosef Kimchi

On Jealousy

How great an ill is jealousy! How sickening a sore! It breaketh the very bones of man, and destroyeth his body soon. Hatred may be kept from view for ever and for aye; but jeaslousy is discerned at once; to all men it is clear.

Thou mayest succeed in pleasing all save him who envieth thee thy riches; for his heart will never be content, till thou hast lost thy happiness and wealth.

Thou canst not find a sinner greater than the man who hateth one to whom honours have come; for continually upon his Creator, he poureth forth his wrath, chafed at what He hath willed as the other man's lot.

On the day thou callest a fool to thy help, thou dost invite him to destroy thee root and branch; for were it not that there are trees in the forest, the axe which is seized by the hand of man would indeed have nothing to hew.

A cure there is for every form of hate, save for the hate that springeth from envy.

The envious one will not have length of days, since he hath neither hope nor expectation; he will grieve, and his grief will be unending, if he find that he can do no further harm unto others.

Envy not one blessed all the days of his life with the enjoyment of pleasure, when thou seest him happy and full of delight, whilst thou art ever full of care and sorrow.

How foolish the spite, the ill-will how petty! Three classes there are whom men envy the most - the men of their craft, their relatives, and their friends, who outstrip them in honour and greatness.

Be thou not envious, and thou shalt rise, and honour gain; thou shalt rejoice and prosper.

Shekel HaKodesh

Rabbi

Yosef Kimchi

On Hypocrisy, Slander, and Evil Neighbors

He who adorneth himself with ornaments which are not proper or right, will live to see the test applied, and the truth will be revealed. If a man deck himself with something far from natural, when least expected he will expose the fleck. Tis just as when a man dyeth his hair, the weak parts which he intends to hide will be sure to tell against him.

Like a fever that spreadeth through the frame of a man the health of his body to spoil, is the companion whose heart is full of ill-will; for while he seeketh to speak of his friend's failures and faults, his good points and merits he taketh care to obscure.

When thou hearest a person reviling thy friend, some failing exposing, or speaking some slander, while thy friend never speaketh a word against him; then draw thy friend closer to thee, and look on the slanderer with horror and scorn, for his way is to speak against men; the wickedness of hatred and baseness of falsehood are the weapons he calleth to aid.

The man once thought trustworthy by thee, who hath been found guilty of slander, trust nevermore his word or oath; for had he been the man worthy of thy trust, he would have been loath ever to utter to another the slanderous and false report.

Have no faith in all that men do say, for untruthful speech is oft the outcome of man's lips; he who trusteth the slanderer who evil tales doth bear, will find ere long he hath neither kin nor a single friend left.

Disclose not that which is bound by friendship's secrecy, lest God the secret things concerning thee reveal.

In spirit be meek, humble, and low, ever shunning all anger and slander; besmirch no man through ill report; know, that the talebearer is oft the tale-maker.

As for him who would thy comrade be, whose heart is ill-disposed, remove from him, keep far away, be never close to him; for while he keepeth hid and concealed the good that thou doest, he taketh care that all thy failings shall well be brought to light.

The bully at all times will hate what is good, and

choose evil, rebellion, and strife; like the fly which seeketh out the wound that is sore, avoiding the spot that is healthy and sound.

The man who endureth the injury done to him by his neighbour, will in time possess that neighbour's house and all of his belongings. The best revenge that man can avenge him of his foe, is to strengthen within him all that's good, and his reward shall dwell with him.

In hating thy fellow, what sins do thy mouth and heart upon thee bring! Tilling, and ploughing, and sowing hate, naught but regret thou shalt reap.

Beware, and treat no man with scorn, nor let him feel thy slight; a tiny fly may choke a man, having seized him by the throat.

Who from an evil companion his distance shall keep, his Rock of Salvation is sure to behold and so the tongue of the slanderer he need never fear.

Shekel HaKodesh

Rabbi

Yosef Kimchi

On Visiting Friends and the Sick, and on Nuisances in Visiting

He who faileth to visit his intimate friend doeth violence to his soul; but he whose dull visit is one heavy wail, will meet with confusion, insult, and shame.

Visit but rarely, attachment will grow; from visits too, frequent estrangement will spring.

Let not a mile be the proverbial stile, when thou shouldst visit the sorrowing and sick; let two miles be as nothing, when as peacemaker thou'rt sought, to cause strife and dissension to cease among men.

Visit not thy friends at all times and all hours but keep back thy foot from their dwelling; see, how men long for the showers of rain, when for a time they are kept back from the earth.

When a bore once came to visit a friend, prolonging

his stay to an inordinate length, the patient remarked - If thou hast business to do, then say so, be quick! Let's be done with the thing! Or if it's a debt thou hast come to claim, then speak of the debt. How much do I owe? I'll give it - Take it and go.

O dullard, if Thou'll be advised for thy good, pray visit the sick no longer; for worse, worse by far than the sickness itself, are the visits that prove thee a bore.

A patient was once asked - What aileth thee? And he answered forthwith - My will, that is stubborn and sinful. They said unto him then - What is the wish that thou wouldst now ask? And he answered and said - My sole wish is that Heaven may forgive me my sins. Again, they did ask - Shall we go and fetch the physician? And he answered and said - Twas he who made me ill. They continued and spake - Shall we give you some relish? And his answer was then - I am sick of all food.

To keep off the bore from thy circle of friends, have little to do with him, give him no ear.

Like tasting of honeycomb's droppings, is the pleasure of dining with friends; to dine with men that are hateful to thee, is as bad as the fever and scab.

When thou seest two in close converse, quickly

withdraw and hold back; obtrude not thyself on their presence.

The world grows sick of the society of those who never cease to prate.

A King, to get rid of the bore he did hate, bethought him of this fine device - He bade them inscribe on the signet he wore these words which bluntly told him his mind - Canst thou not see thou art a great bore? O dull one, rise and begone. And this ring he would turn again and again, till the bore rose up and went off.

Is it not writ in the 8th and 9th chapters of Medical Lore, that, as the quaternary fever is the visit of the heavy and dull?

When a dull man visiteth thee at one time or another, and, stupidly chatting on a host of things, repeateth himself in his talk, then make thyself deaf, and pretend to be blind, act as though thou hast lost the use of thy feet, and as though thy mouth, in rebellion, had resolved not to speak.

Visit a friend, visit the sick; but pray, cease thou from visiting at all, if thou must needs be heavy and dull.

Shekel HaKodesh

Rabbi

Yosef Kimchi

Last Chapter of the Book; Collection of Maxims

Before the tyrant or ruler shed not thy tears, for not alone will he mock thee, but he will also despise thee; so, to the man without troubles reveal not thy sorrow, askance he'll look at thee, or he may not even regard thee.

Be ready to seek advice from all, whether they be young or old; at times thou mightest think it well to act on advice that cometh from a boor.

Reside in the place where thy fathers have dwelt and set up thy dwelling in their old habitation; there's a place in the world for all who would dwell in it; e'en the bird nestles best in its own favourite nest.

To a woman a secret thou shouldst never disclose, lest for thy pains it brings thee derision; if thou dost prize dearly the life that is thine, quaff not the poison, it's too great a trial.

He who entrusteth his possessions to his child or to his wife, will sure come to beggary, having first come to shame.

He that chideth him who refuseth to take sound advice, who speaketh to hearts that are closed, is like one who singeth a song to the dead, or crieth in prayer to the shades.

The man of sense needs but few words whereby he may profit, and be corrected; understanding well, he will see the purpose of things; he will fix them deep within his heart and grasp them from end to end.

The man always laughing is a fool, and for his folly there is no cure and relief; at the time when he showeth his teeth, he loseth his dignity and honour.

Take a long time to make up thy mind, and then shall thy actions be perfectly sound; for the garden-fruit that is late in appearing will always be sweeter and far more mature.

Spend not thy strength, O wise one, in the attempt to overcome the wicked; but being strong and all-daring, oppose a bold front; for oft in his net the victor will fall, and the conquered will truly the conqueror be named.

In speaking, a stupid man will send his tongue in advance of his good sense; but a man of sense will check his tongue, and let prudence keep it back.

The fool in mischief findeth his sport; hence his reason cometh after his tongue; but the man of sense delayeth his words, and beginneth no matter until he hath grasped it.

He who promiseth a gift from day to day, sickeneth the heart with hope deferred; as the lowering clouds, that rainless pass, cover the face of the earth with gloom.

If thy soul shall fulness have, and poverty thou dost fear, then turn about, and take advice, and show thyself truly wise - of food take less, and duly shun the vice of gluttony; how little meat for proper folk will readily suffice! Too many wives, in the next place, see that thou dost avoid, and be on thy guard, lest thou dost sin, and thy strength unto strangers give. Whene'er thy soul desireth some object to attain, think, is not the price thou pay'st for it much too high and dear? Surely it is better by far to leave of thy riches to thy foes, than, recklessly spending all that thou hast, to beg cold charity of the wealthy.

When kindly fortune waiteth on man, the very stones on the road shall yield him bdellium and gold; and if it be destined that he shall succeed, the branch that is dry shall blossom in his hand; be assured and believe that on the day he doth sow, beautiful branches will bud and spring forth.

If thou listen to counsel, thou'lt shine forth bright, and thy soul shall be at ease with herself, finding favour with all.

Finished with the help of God. Blessed be He who giveth power to the weary, and to him who hath no strength He increaseth strength.